# NARROW GAUGE
# IN THE AMERICAS

## by James Waite

Published by Mainline & Maritime Ltd, 3 Broadleaze, Upper Seagry, near Chippenham, SN15 5EY
Tel: 07770 748615 www.mainlineandmaritime.co.uk orders@mainlineandmaritime.co.uk
Printed in the UK

ISBN: 978-1-900340-72-4    © Mainline & Maritime Ltd, & Author 2020

**Front Cover:** On 22 February 2017 Southern Pacific 4-6-0 no 18 (Baldwin 37395/1918) heads a short freight train away from Laws station in eastern California. To the left are water and fuel oil tanks and a turntable, and the tall cream-coloured building is a water pumphouse which dates from the railway's very early years. Alas, no 18 didn't have far to run as only 600 yards of track remain at what is now a museum devoted to the old line.

**Above:** The 3ft gauge Eureka & Palisade RR's no 4 EUREKA (Baldwin 3763/1875) at a level crossing midway along the Boulder City museum's short 3ft gauge line on 15 December 2018.

**Back Cover:** The 750mm gauge railway through Patagonia runs within sight of the Andes mountains for much of its length south of El Maitén, roughly midway along the route.  Here is 2-8-2 no 4 (Baldwin 55432/1922) near Leleque on 22 October 2014.

# INTRODUCTION

Welcome to this second photo album being produced to assist the Talyllyn Railway during the Covid-19 pandemic. This time the subjects are narrow gauge steam railways in the Americas in the twenty first century.

Inevitably most space has been devoted to heritage railways in the US. Narrow gauge construction began there in 1870 when the first section of the Rio Grande system was built south from Denver. Its founder, General William Jackson Palmer, chose the 3ft gauge. He was influenced by the Ffestiniog and added the extra foot or so to take account of the generally more open conditions in much of the Rocky Mountains through which it would run. Within a few years 3ft railways were being built throughout almost the entire country, and the gauge went on to be adopted for several railways in Central America and as far south as Colombia.

The main exception in the US was in the northeastern state of Maine. In 1877 George E Mansfield, another disciple of the Ffestiniog, built the Billerica & Bedford RR, a pioneering 2ft gauge line in eastern Massachusetts. It wasn't a commercial success and closed the following year, but its equipment found a second home on the Sandy River RR in Maine. By the early 1900s several more 2ft gauge railways had been built in the state.

The Rio Grande went on to become an important standard gauge railway for transcontinental traffic and its 3ft system ended up as something of a backwater. The last section closed in 1968 with one exception, the scenic Durango to Silverton branch which had become effectively a tourist railway. By then almost every other narrow gauge line throughout the country had either closed or been converted to standard gauge, but the Silverton branch pointed to a new future. The mainline east of Durango ran through districts of considerable poverty. The Rio Grande had been almost the only employer in many of the districts through which it ran and the hardship became even more dire after its staff were laid off. To help alleviate it the states of Colorado and New Mexico reopened the most mountainous section as the Cumbres & Toltec Scenic RR in 1971.

In the UK we rightly regard the Talyllyn as the world's first preserved railway. It was rescued by enthusiasts from almost certain closure when its owner died in 1950 but it's worth remembering that in the US the private preservation and operation of locos and rolling stock, though not the rescue of complete railways, began several years earlier. The Sandy River & Rangeley Lakes RR, formed by the amalgamation of the Sandy River and other 2ft gauge lines in Franklin County in Maine, closed in 1935. Its loss acted as a wakeup call to many US enthusiasts, just as the closure of the Lynton & Barnstaple in the same year did in the UK. The many fine steam locos still on the line were scrapped with almost indecent haste, but it also ran a number of i/c-powered railcars. Edgar T Mead, an enthusiast from New Hampshire, bought one and presented it to the Bridgton & Harrison, another Maine 2-footer, to help it reduce costs and, he hoped, to save it for the future.

He wasn't alone. In 1937 a group of enthusiasts bought a 0-4-4 Forney tank loco from the Wiscasset, Waterville & Farmington RR, another Maine 2-footer, which had closed in 1933. They planned to set up a tourist railway, though in the event this didn't come to pass and the loco was to remain in store for some sixty years. In the following year Ward and Betty Kimball bought a coach when passenger services ended on the Southern Pacific's narrow gauge line in eastern California, soon followed by a 2-6-0 from the Nevada Central RR. By 1942 they had built the Grizzly Flats RR in the garden of their home in San Gabriel, California. Mr Kimball was an animator with the Walt Disney company. Mr Disney, a personal friend, was a visitor and was inspired first to build a miniature railway in his own garden, and later to include a 3ft gauge railway at his first theme park in California, which opened in 1955. With more than six million visitors annually it has gone on to become possibly the most popular tourist railway anywhere in the world. Other 3ft railways have followed as his company has opened more parks elsewhere.

Up in Maine the Bridgton & Harrison closed in 1941, notwithstanding Mr Mead's efforts. There was a failed attempt by enthusiasts to take it over but hostility from the Bridgton local authority, which owned it, was too great, and the world had to wait another nine years before the rescue of the Talyllyn showed what could be done. However, all was not lost. Much of the stock, including Mr Mead's railcar, was bought by an enthusiast named Ellis D Atwood from southern Massachusetts, where he operated the largest privately-run cranberry plantation anywhere in the world. He planned to build a railway to provide essential transport for the cranberries and the people who harvested them, as well as being a live museum of the Maine 2-footers. Restrictions during the Second World War meant that he couldn't make immediate progress, but as soon as peace returned he enlisted the services of Linwood Moody, a railwayman at Portland, Maine, who had fallen in love with his state's 2ft lines back in the 1930s. The two men set up the Edaville Railroad. Tracklaying began in earnest in the autumn of 1946. By the following summer it was largely complete with more than six miles of route, and was up and running as the first enthusiast-run railway anywhere in the world.

The two extensive sections of the old Rio Grande narrow gauge which were saved after the closure in 1968 weren't the first 3ft lines to be preserved. The East Broad Top RR, the last-surviving 3ft gauge common carrier in the east of the US, closed in 1956 and was sold to a scrap metal concern headed by one Nick Covalchick. To everyone's surprise the line, its locos and its rolling stock remained in situ and four years later Mr Kovalchick reopened a section as a heritage railway. Further south the 3ft gauge East Tennessee and Western North Carolina RR closed in 1950. Enthusiasts from Virginia purchased one of its last locos and some of its coaches, helped by the railway's management which sold them for much less than their scrap value. The Virginian venture failed but in 1957 the loco moved to a newly-opened theme park close to the old line's eastern terminus, and has operated there ever since.

Far away in Alaska and northwestern Canada the White Pass & Yukon RR couldn't survive the opening in 1972 of a main road which ran parallel to its route. Fortunately it wasn't immediately dismantled, and the rapid development of cruise ship traffic along Alaska's Pacific coast led to the reopening of a section as a tourist railway six years later. Elsewhere an increasing awareness of their historical significance has seen the reconstruction of sections of long-lost railways right across the country while other lines have been built from scratch. They have in common the use of historic equipment, a surprising amount of which has survived.

Further south tentative steps towards the establishment of heritage railways and services in Central America did not stand the test of time, and for the past few years there have been no working steam locos there. Things are altogether happier in Colombia. A steam service running out of Bogotá survived the complete closure of the country's railway system with only a brief interruption. Today's Turistren operation is hugely successful, and is greatly valued by Bogotános and people from much further afield.

Enthusiasts in Brazil took the first steps towards the rescue of locos and rolling stock in the late 1960s. The first heritage railway opened for business in 1984 and there are now several successful operations. Ecuador's state railway is also actively involved in conservation. I have not yet visited and the superbly scenic FC Guayaquil and Quito through the Andes mountains, and also the sugar railways in Cuba, are perhaps the major omissions from this book. Argentina's enthusiast community has rescued many locos and pieces of rolling stock, mainly in and around Buenos Aires, and the country's only heritage railway, down in a remote part of Patagonia, owes much to the determination of its local authorities to encourage tourism and local employment. There are other well-run heritage ventures up and down South America, from a fine museum of Venezuela's railways in the north to the preservation, and occasional operation, of a remote 2ft gauge sand quarry railway in Uruguay - complete with all its twenty six steam locos! In a continent where passenger railways are largely things of the past all these initiatives are very welcome and deserve the support and encouragement of enthusiasts everywhere.

This book wouldn't have been possible without the help of many kind people. In particular I must thank James Patten for his help at the WW&F, Chris Robbins at Tweetsie, James Bane at the Sumpter Valley, Dan Markoff, Brian Norden and Wendell Huffman at the Nevada museums and Daniel Osborne at the Tanana Valley. Pepe Fabregat was very welcoming in México and was distressed that the steaming of NdeM no 279 went wrong at the last minute. In El Salvador Ing Salvador Sanabria Mira, his assistant Mrs Ingrid de Ceseña and the Fenedesal staff at San Salvador were overwhelmingly kind and hospitable. Bruno Sanches, Julio Moraes, Leandro Guidini and Dr José Warmuth went out of their way to help me in Brazil as did Steve Cossey and Eduardo Rodriguez in Colombia, and Richard Campbell was equally helpful in Argentina. To them and to many others whom I have not named I wholeheartedly offer my thanks.

In tackling this wide-ranging subject I have drawn on information from many books, magazine articles and internet pages and without their authors' work this book would not have been possible. A list of them all would occupy far too much space in a relatively small book and in place of individual acknowledgements hope that their authors will accept this collective note of thanks.

Although I have tried to concentrate on photos of trains in action there are inevitably some static ones, particularly in places where it's a long time since the trains have run. It seems to me that heritage involves conservation and wherever possible I have tried to present scenes which look something like they would have done when the trains were running for real – though there are some very obvious exceptions! I've arranged the photos to present a virtual journey from east to west across the USA and Canada and then on south through Central and South America. Climb on board, sit back and enjoy the ride!

*James Waite*

0-4-4 Forney tank no 9 (Portland 624/1891) is the only surviving loco from the old Wiscasset, Waterville and Farmington Railway. She was built for the Sandy River RR in western Maine, and went on to serve the Sandy River & Rangeley Lakes and, from 1924, the Kennebec Central until arriving at the WW&F early in 1933, only a few months before the derailment of another loco led to its closure. Enter Harry Percival who had lived beside the old trackbed for many years and was determined to resuscitate a part of the line. In 1985 he bought much of its route and the title to the original operating company, and built his home at the old Sheepscot station. In 1989 the WW&F museum society was born. Now enthusiasts have rebuilt about three miles of the railway and more is set to follow. Here no 9 shunts at Sheepscot station on the preserved section of the line on 14 January 2017. With her is Monson RR 0-4-4T no 3 (Vulcan Iron Works 2093/1912), visiting from her home at the Maine Narrow Gauge Railroad Museum in Portland.

Nos 9 and 3 stand at Top o' the Mountain, then the northern terminus of the revived section of the WW&F, on 14 January 2017. The Monson RR had become the last surviving Maine 2-footer before it closed in 1944. It was comprehensively scrapped almost at once and Mr Moody was surprised to discover two years later that instead of dismantling the locos the scrapmen had taken them to their yard at Rochester in New York state. They were promptly acquired for Edaville.

No 3 climbs the bank leading to Alna Center station with a southbound train on 15 January 2017. This was perhaps what scenes on the old Monson line looked like with the dense pine woodland which characterises much of Maine, save that the Monson only ever possessed one coach! It was six miles long, together with a two-mile mineral extension to reach the slate quarry which provided most of its traffic – all rather like the Talyllyn!

The railway which became the WW&F opened in 1895 as the grandly-named Wiscasset & Quebec, but its mainline never reached further than twenty eight miles beyond Wiscasset, a small port on the estuary of the Sheepscot River in Maine. Financial reconstructions brought the less ambitious name by which it has been known ever since; one of them involved a takeover by no less a person than the vice-president of the FW Woolworth company. The W&Q's coach no 3 was built by Jackson & Sharp of Wilmington, Delaware in 1894 in time for the opening. In the early 1900s it was sold to the Bridgton & Saco River RR, a predecessor of the Bridgton & Harrison, and it went on to be rescued by Ellis Atwood for Edaville in 1941. It is the only survivor of the old WW&F's coaches and is now back on its old line. Here no 9 shunts it at Sheepscot on 14 January 2017.

On 14 January 2017 no 9 stands on the newly-built wooden turntable at Sheepscot, a replica of the one which stood at the old railway's Wiscasset depot. In 1937 no 9, flatcar no 118 and boxcar no 309 moved to a farm owned by Frank Ramsdell, one of the enthusiasts who rescued her, and were later looked after by his daughter Alice. Mr Atwood knew that the Ramsdells had become very fond of the loco and didn't press them to let him have her for Edaville. Harry Percival befriended Alice, and she allowed him to provide a home at Sheepscot for flatcar no 118 which duly became the first piece of stock to return to the line. On her death in 1994 the loco and the boxcar passed to her nephew Dale King, who generously allowed them to follow no 118 to Sheepscot. The coach partly visible on the left was built for the Bridgton & Saco River and was another one saved by Mr Atwood.

This pretty little loco, Vulcan Iron Works 574/1904, is reminiscent of the small 0-4-4 Forney tank locos built for the WW&F and for other Maine 2-footers in their earliest years, but she was 2ft 6ins gauge and was supplied to the Belleview sugar plantation far away in southern Louisiana. She moved around over the years, ending her Louisiana days at the Westfield Plantation in Paincourtville in 1958, after which she was acquired for Edaville and converted to 2ft gauge. Very sadly Mr Atwood was killed by a boiler explosion at his cranberry processing plant in 1950. The Edaville RR continued to flourish, but in later years a decline set in and it closed in 1992. The four locos which had come from Maine returned to the state, but this one remained at Edaville until 1999 when she was sold to the WW&F society to become their no 10. She arrived in full working order and took charge of most trains until no 9's rebuild was completed late in 2015. Shortly afterwards major problems became apparent which require construction of a new boiler and the loco is currently stored out of use. Back in happier days she was approaching Alna Center with a southbound train on 4 September 2014. The leading coach is one built at Edaville in traditional style after rising visitor numbers outstripped the capacity of the coaches from Maine.

The Maine locos at Edaville and many of the coaches were bought by the newly-formed museum at Portland. Until very recently it has been based at the historic Portland Company's factory, on Portland's waterfront, which had been the birthplace of WW&F no 9. The factory building can just be seen in this photo of Monson RR no 4 (Vulcan Iron Works 2780/1918) in the late afternoon of 22 October 2011.

Recently the arrangement for the use of the old loco factory has come to an end and the building's future is now most uncertain. The museum operates a line rather more than one mile in length along the waterfront. Here no 4's work is over for the day and she approaches the engine shed on 22 October 2011. It is hoped to build new premises at the far end of the line and in the meantime many of the locos and stock are housed temporarily at the WW&F. No 4 now needs major overhaul but this is unlikely to begin until the new building has been completed.

Not all the Maine 2-footers were public railways. The SD Warren paper factory at Westbrook, in the western outskirts of Portland, operated a large 2ft gauge system. It was established in 1867 and was worked by horses until 0-4-0ST no 1 (Baldwin 14283/1895) arrived. A sister loco, no 2, arrived later that year. No 3, another Baldwin, came in 1905 but in later years was dismantled to provide spares for nos 1 and 2. A fourth loco was built by Davenport in 1914 but her fate isn't clear. Nos 1 and 2 worked until the system closed in 1949 and they were sold to a theme park in New Jersey. Since 1961 they have been preserved at the Boothbay Railway Village which lies a few miles down the Sheepscot estuary from Wiscasset. In 2018 no 2 was restored to working order. Here's no 1 on 22 October 2014, at the head of a display consisting of a boxcar no 312 built in 1894 for the Wiscasset & Quebec, two more boxcars both built in 1912 for the Sandy River & Rangeley Lakes and a superb combine coach built by the Laconia Car Company in 1885 for the Franklin & Megantic, a constituent of the SR&RL.

The Edaville RR was revived in 1999, paradoxically at much the same time as the sale of the Louisiana loco to the WW&F. The Maine locos had long gone, but two of the eleven 2ft 6ins gauge 0-4-0STs built by Porter for the Raritan Copper Works at Perth Amboy in New Jersey had been bought for static display in 1959 and were still there. No 11 (Porter 6976/1925) was rebuilt at the Boothbay's shops as a 2ft gauge 0-4-0 tender loco between 2012 and 2014. On 4 September 2014 she takes a train away from Thorndike station at Boothbay while running in before her return to Edaville. The fine building to the right dates from 1871, and graced a standard gauge station in Maine before being rescued by the village, one of whose principal functions is to provide a new home for attractive old buildings which were no longer loved in their previous locations. No 11 is hardly a historically accurate loco but I thought she made a pretty picture, and should be included out of respect for the vital contribution which Edaville made towards the preservation of the Maine 2-footers and the heritage railway movement more generally.

Here's no 11 again, climbing the steep hill on Boothbay's railway on 4 September 2014. The leading coach is another one from the Franklin & Megantic.

Christmas train! The 3ft gauge East Tennessee and Western North Carolina RR (what a long name!) and the associated Linville Valley Railway ran through the Blue Ridge Mountains, and acquired the nickname *Tweetsie* after the sound of its locos' whistles. Its first section, from a junction with the Southern Railway at Johnson City in Tennessee, opened in 1881, and in 1918 the line reached Boone, sixty four miles away in the hills of North Carolina. On the way it passed through a mining district at Cranberry, and the transport of its product was one of the principal reasons for its construction. Here 4-6-0 no 12 (Baldwin 45069/1917), its last surviving narrow gauge loco, passes over a level crossing at the Tweetsie Railroad theme park near Boone, at dusk on 14 December 2018. She is one of seven 4-6-0s built for the line, the five survivors of which worked most traffic on the old railway for many years. During the Second World War two of them were requisitioned by the US army for service on the White Pass & Yukon Railway in Alaska and northwestern Canada. It had become the principal route for military supplies after Japanese forces occupied some of the Aleutian Islands and it was feared that they might move on to attack or invade the continental US. The locos were scrapped at the end of the war, and Tweetsie had to rely on its three remaining 4-6-0s for its narrow gauge services in their final years.

The district which Tweetsie served suffered badly during the 1930s depression. To cheer things up the railway repainted its locos green with gold lining, copied from the Southern which in turn had reportedly copied the colour from the UK's Southern Railway, and added embellishments including red chimney caps and numberplates and aluminium-coloured edges to the wheel tyres. The theme park's line runs for a little under three miles around the Roundhouse Mountain. There are steep gradients and no 12 has to work hard for her living. The blizzards which had swept through the Blue Ridge Mountains during the previous few days had turned to heavy rain, but this didn't deter the large numbers of people who turned out for an evening ride on Tweetsie. The trains were full and here no 12 passes a few hardy visitors out along the lineside on 14 December 2018. In the foreground are some open hearths on which toasted marshmallows were being offered, a popular treat in the US.

The last narrow gauge train ran in 1950, though the eleven miles between Johnson City and Elizabethton had been converted to mixed gauge as long ago as 1906 and continued to operate until the early years of the twenty first century – and a few sidings at Johnson City are still in use. 4ft 8½ins was the third gauge which the railway used because its first section was built as a 5ft gauge line, which was graced by an elegant large-wheeled 4-4-0 which made a few runs but which it possibly did not actually own. However it never opened until it was rebuilt as a 3-footer. Enthusiasts from Virginia saved no 12, helped by Tweetsie's management who sold her for much less than her scrap value. They built a heritage railway but it didn't last long and in 1957 local businessman Grover Robbins stepped in. He bought the loco and to the delight of many residents set up the present theme park in the outskirts of Blowing Rock, a town which straddles the Eastern Continental Divide a few miles south of Boone. No 12 was working hard on 14 December 2018. The snow made for a classic Christmas scene, though ice on the main road up to Boone made for very difficult driving conditions!

Away from the station the snow was, if anything, even deeper and there were illuminated displays all along the line. The good people of North Carolina certainly know how to celebrate Christmas in style! The coaches are approximate copies of four vehicles which the old Tweetsie line built between 1911 and 1917, some or all of which were probably converted from freight cars. The railway ran through the spectacular Doe River Gorge, which was about 1,000 feet deep in places from the tops of the rocks to the river, and tourist traffic became important after the turn of the century. Jackson & Sharp built some smart corridor coaches in the 1910s and early 1920s, the first on a 3ft gauge line anywhere in the US. Finest of all was a parlour car named AZALEA with a particularly magnificent brass-railed end balcony. Sadly seven of the best coaches were sold in the aftermath of the 1930s depression. Most are believed to have gone to the United Fruit Company for its banana railways in Central America, though a photo exists of a first class coach lettered FCNdeM which perhaps stood for the Ferrocarriles Nacionales de México, the country's state-owned railway. Some were reported to have been converted in Tweetsie's shops at Johnson City to 3ft 6ins gauge and these would probably have been for United Fruit's railways in Honduras or Costa Rica. AZALEA became VOLCAN on the 3ft system in western Panama run by the Chiriquí Land Company, a United Fruit subsidiary. 14 December 2018.

No 12's driver checks around the loco before she sets off for another trip on 14 December 2018. Since 1960 no 12 has been helped by a MacArthur-type 2-8-2 which was built for the US army's operations on the White Pass line. After Tweetsie's standard gauge line changed from steam to diesel in 1967 much of the specialised machinery in the Johnson City shops began a new life at the theme park. In 1997 it opened a state-of-the-art 5,000 square feet shop which not only maintains its own locos to a high standard but also carries out contract steam work for many other railways. The theme park's line isn't the only Tweetsie-related railway on which visitors can ride. A section of the old route through the Doe River Gorge was rebuilt in the 1960s and today forms an integral part of a Christian youth camp. It is only lightly constructed and suitable for small locos and speeders but it would be well worth asking to visit if in the district during the summer.

The company which built the 3ft gauge East Broad Top RR was chartered in 1856, but construction was delayed by the US civil war and it didn't open until 1871. Its principal traffic was coal from mines on the eastern side of Broad Top Mountain. The driving force behind its construction was one Ario Pardee junior. His family was involved in both the Broad Top mines and those at Cranberry, North Carolina, and he was also a promoter of the Tweetsie line. The two companies shared at least one board member for the whole of their existence. EBT outlived Tweetsie's narrow gauge operations by only six years and became the last-surviving common carrier 3-footer in the east of the US when they ended in 1950. After the reopening under Mr Kovalchick in 1960 it operated until 2011, and very late in the evening of 6 October that year its 2-8-2 no 15 (Baldwin 41196/1914) raises steam in its roundhouse at Rockhill Furnace. Behind her is 2-8-2 no 14 (Baldwin 38625/1912).

It sounds like a cliché but almost everything about the EBT is something of a time warp from the golden days of narrow gauge railroading in the US. One superb example is its magnificent business car no 20 Orbisonia, complete with period leather-upholstered armchairs. It was built by the Billmeyer and Small Car Works in 1882, and came to the EBT in 1907 second hand from the Big Level and Kinzua RR. Here it stands at Orbisonia station on the evening of 8 October 2011.

The EBT was sufficiently profitable to enable the main line to be upgraded and relaid with heavier rail in the early 1900s. This facilitated the use of much larger locos than had been common on many of the country's narrow gauge lines. The first loco fitted with a trailing truck, 2-6-2 no 11, arrived from Baldwin in 1908 and six 2-8-2s followed from 1911. In this view looking out from the Rockhill Furnace roundhouse early in the morning of 8 October 2011 no 15 is being prepared for her day's work. The tender on the right belongs to no 18 (Baldwin 53545/1920), the youngest of the 2-8-2s. After no 11 was withdrawn in 1943 they were responsible for all its loco-hauled operations.

Another view of no 15 out in the early morning sunshine at Rockhill Furnace on 8 October 2011. 2-8-2 no 17 (Baldwin 48075/1918) stands on the right, and petrol railcar no M-1, built by the EBT in 1927 from parts supplied by the JG Brill company, has just entered the scene on the left. It was one of three railcars on the line. M-2 was built by Tweetsie in 1924 for a suburban service between Johnson City and Elizabethton, but road improvements and a new bus service soon rendered the service impracticable and in 1926 the railcar was sold to the EBT. It wasn't liked there and disappeared two years later. In 1928 the EBT built M-3, a much smaller inspection vehicle using parts from a Nash motorcar. It's still very much an active vehicle at the railway.

The period from around 1910 to the early 1930's saw what were perhaps the line's golden years. An initial order for 10 large all-steel bogie coal hoppers in 1913 from the Pressed Steel Car Co was followed by more than two hundred similar vehicles which were built in the company's own shops at Rockhill Furnace. A few have been restored to running condition and here no 15 heads north from Orbisonia on 7 October 2011 with a train which includes some of them.

On 7 October 2011 no 15 approaches McMullen's summit, the highest point on the old railway between its headquarters at Orbisonia and its junction with the Pennsylvania RR at Mount Union. The line remained dormant from late 2011 until February 2020 when the welcome news arrived that it had been sold to a non-profit group led by well-respected professional railwaymen. They intend to reopen a first section in 2021 and, despite the Covid-19 outbreak, have already made good progress towards implementing their plans.

No 15 has passed the summit and the fireman is preparing her for the downhill run to Orbisonia on 7 October 2011. The coal dust and slack in the leading hopper wagon look unfit for any purpose!

No 15 takes her train over Blacklog Creek as she approaches Orbisonia station on 7 October 2011. Large numbers of hopper wagons lay unused after 1956 and many still slumber in the undergrowth to this day. Others have proved a godsend to many of the country's heritage railways for permanent way work and can be seen as far away as Indiana, Colorado, Oregon and Alaska. Some provided the chassis on which the Tweetsie theme park's carriages were built.

There's more of the EBT's historic infrastructure in this photo of no 15 as she stands behind the large range of wooden buildings which house its workshops on 8 October 2011. The stub point and the harp point lever are amongst the very few survivors of their type in the US, or anywhere else in the world. Inside the shops is a wealth of old shaft- and belt-driven machinery powered by stationary steam engines. Little of it has been operable in recent years since subsidence has pushed many of the shafts out of true. The new regime intends to stabilise the buildings and restore the machinery to working order.

2-8-2s nos 18 and 16 (Baldwin 43562/1916) look out from the back of the roundhouse on 8 October 2011. They've been doing this ever since the old railway closed in 1956 as neither has ever been restored to working order. The new regime has carried out a thorough survey of all the locos and no 16, along with no 14, has been chosen to be the first to be returned to traffic.

This elaborate decoration adorns the interior of the roof of EBT coach no 8. Like several on the line the coach came second hand from the Boston, Revere Beach and Lynn RR. In the 1920's it was fitted with roller bearings for use as a trailer with railcar M-1.

2-8-2 no 12 (Baldwin 37325/1911) and no 15 stand at Orbisonia station in the evening of 7 October 2011. No 12, the oldest of the six 2-8-2s, had been out of service for several years but was spruced up for this photographic session to mark her 100th anniversary.

On 23 May 2014 Rio Grande K-27 class 2-8-2 no 463 (Baldwin 21788/1903) and C-18 class 2-8-0 no 315 (Baldwin 14352/1895), originally numbered 425, stand outside Antonito engine shed, at the eastern end of the Cumbres & Toltec Scenic RR, one of the two preserved sections of the Rio Grande's 3ft gauge. They were being prepared to work the line's first westbound train of the season on the following day. The fifteen K-27s were the Rio Grande's first 2-8-2s and were originally Vauclain compounds, but were rebuilt as simples between 1907 and 1909.

A view from the train on 24 May 2014 as nos 463 and 315 head away from Antonito. No 463 is one of two surviving K-27s. She was withdrawn in the early 1950s and was on display at Antonito for many years after 1971 until being restored to working order, making her first trip in 1994. She suffered a broken side rod in 2002 and didn't return to service until 2013. No 315, originally no 3 ELKTON of the Florence & Cripple Creek RR, arrived on the Rio Grande in 1917 after her old line closed, and worked until 1949. She was restored by volunteers after many years of static display at Durango and first ran again in 2007.

Early in the morning of 25 May 2014 K-36 class 2-8-2 no 488 (Baldwin 58589/1925) has steam up at Chama engine shed at the western end of the C&TS. She had been repainted over the winter and was preparing to make her first journey of the season. The K-36s were much larger and more powerful than any previous locos on the Rio Grande narrow gauge, though they were rather less expensive to buy than the ten K-28 class 2-8-2s supplied by Alco two years earlier.

K-36 no 489 (Baldwin 58590/1925) and no 463 stand at Chama engine shed on 25 May 2014. Back in Rio Grande days the shed was one of several on the system designated as helper sheds, in the case of Chama to provide banking or pilot assistance on the steep climb to Cumbres summit at an altitude of 10,016 feet. For most of their lives the K-36s regularly saw service on the Alamosa-Durango railway, of which the C&TS forms the central part, and they also worked on the Rio Grande's principal narrow gauge lines further north until they closed in the 1950s.

On 21 September 2011 no 489, temporarily renumbered 485, climbs towards Cumbres summit on the C&TS. Ten K-36s were built in 1925, and all have survived apart from no 485 which was scrapped after falling into a turntable pit at Salida in 1953. Nos 483-4 and 487-9 are on the C&TS. They are usually kept in working order and work most trains over the line, except for no 483 which hasn't run for many years.

No 489 (alias 485) approaches Coxo level crossing on 21 September 2011. Her temporary renumbering wasn't as fanciful as one might think as many of no 485's parts were salvaged and reused during an overhaul of no 489 at the Rio Grande's Salida shops, the last one to be carried out there on a K-36. They were very much in situ when the C&TS first overhauled the loco and some are probably still there now, though the number of original parts on all these locos is declining as newly-manufactured replacements are fitted.

The railway from Chama to Cumbres takes a circuitous route above Coxo crossing in order to climb up the western flank of the rocky outcrop called Windy Point. This photo, taken from the crossing, shows no 489 as she climbs past the rocks and approaches the summit on 21 September 2011.

Another view from Coxo of no 489 and her train at Windy Point on 21 September 2011.

Just after sunrise on 22 September 2011 no 487 approaches Crespo with a freight train. The region is noted for its autumn colours and they are just beginning to put in an appearance. In 1939 the Rio Grande herald, with its sloping letters, was introduced to replace the older lettering as seen on nos 315, 463 and 478 in these photos. The original standards instruction from the Chief Mechanical Officer required that the letters should lean towards the back of the tender on each side. However the draftsman who prepared the drawing to illustrate the new herald mistakenly showed the letters leaning forwards, and this is how they were almost universally applied.

A view from the rear of this long train as it climbed from Chama towards Cumbres on 22 September 2011. The black-painted vehicles are stock cars in US-parlance, or cattle wagons to us British enthusiasts.

No 487 stands at the cattle pens at Osier station, well to the east of Cumbres, on 22 September 2011. They were still mostly intact though it must have been about fifty years or more since they had last served their intended purpose. Cows had been brought back on this occasion and the intention was to give them a ride to Chama. However, they had other ideas and resolutely refused to board the train. Eventually we set off without them.

No 487 heads west and crosses a timber trestle bridge over the Rio de los Pinos on 22 September 2011.

No 487 stands beneath the splendid wooden coaling stage at Chama on 21 September 2011. The discovery of oil around Farmington, southwest of Durango, kept the old line busy in its final Rio Grande years with the transport of pipeline equipment. Without this traffic it would probably have closed several years earlier. Services ceased promptly after the pipeline was completed in 1968, fortunately at a time of growing awareness of the tourist potential of scenic railways. Had the line not lasted so long it is doubtful that the C&TS would ever have been set up.

Chama engine shed is a hive of activity in the evening as the locos which have arrived are put to bed and those rostered for the next day's train are prepared. Photographers have always been made very welcome there. Here are nos 463 and 488 on 24 May 2014. In addition to being rebuilt as simples several K-27s were modernised with piston valves and superheaters. Two, nos 458 and 459, were sold to NdeM in 1941 as their nos 400 and 401. They were the last narrow gauge steam locos which NdeM acquired and in 1949 were rebuilt to standard gauge, becoming nos 2250 and 2251. One of them remained in traffic until 1962, as did Rio Grande no 464 which was kept on to shunt at Durango. All the others were withdrawn between 1939 and 1957.

A steamy view inside the engine shed and workshops at Chama with nos 489 and 484 in the evening of 24 May 2014. As I write this the C&TS is preparing to celebrate the fiftieth anniversary of its reopening as a tourist railway. It has succeeded admirably in promoting tourism and alleviating unemployment in the district which it serves.

The other surviving K-27 is no 464 (Baldwin 21796/1903) which lives on the Huckleberry RR in Michigan, far away from Rio Grande territory. After retiring as the Durango shunter she went on display there for eleven years and then moved to the Knott's Berry theme park in Buena Vista, California before arriving in Michigan in 1981. The Huckleberry line was built in 1976 by the local authority at Flint, then one of the centres of Michigan's automotive industry, to provide an imaginative leisure facility for its citizens. It uses the trackbed of a standard gauge railway which had closed the previous year, and was one of many cultural and recreational initiatives undertaken at the town which was enjoying a period of considerable prosperity, though this would soon come to an end. Now the car factories have closed and Flint has become an extreme example of a rustbelt community. However the railway and the open air museum of which it is a part, another place which provides a second home for interesting but redundant buildings, are all the more appreciated. Here no 464 and her train cross a creek east of Genesee Village on 15 January 2019.

After the remainder of the railway closed in 1968 the Rio Grande continued to run tourist trains over the Durango-Silverton branch until they sold it in 1981 to Charles Bradshaw junior, a Florida citrus fruit grower. He rebranded the line as the Durango & Silverton Narrow Gauge RR, and upgraded it in order to accommodate the K-36s which today work most trains. Previously the K-28s were the only locos allowed to run over the section beyond Rockwood after the 2-8-0s and the K-27s had been withdrawn. Originally there were ten K-28s, but seven were requisitioned by the US army during the Second World War for service on the White Pass line, and were scrapped when the war ended. The remaining three allowed little scope to expand the services as Mr Bradshaw deemed essential, and so the line's upgrading became central to his plans. Here K-28 no 478 (Alco 64989/1923) heads through a meadow close to the River Animas near what was once Cascade siding. 24 September 2011.

A view from the train on its way back to Durango on 24 September 2011, as no 478 runs alongside the river which keeps the line company for most of its distance. For a few years around 2010 four of the railway's coaches ran in the dark green colour which the Rio Grande, in common with most US railways, used for many years after 1917.

No 478 stands at the splendid old Needleton water tank on 24 September 2011. The tank has been replaced by a more utilitarian structure nearby and no longer holds water, but trains still stop here for photos on special occasions.

The Durango & Silverton runs through some breathtakingly beautiful scenery. This spot, a little to the east of Rockwood station at the entrance to a horseshoe curve on what the D&S calls the High Line, is rightly celebrated as one of the most spectacular locations on any railway, though whether it is any more so than Tweetsie's line through the Doe River Gorge far away in east Tennesee is something of a moot point. On 23 September 2011 no 478 was returning light to Durango after piloting a heavy train up the valley.

Here is another view of no 478 at the horseshoe curve on 23 September 2011. While the rockface above the line is dramatic the sheer drop down to the river 400 feet below is, if anything, even more so. While I was there a bald eagle came into view – one of the country's most emblematic birds. Most of them only pass over Colorado while migrating in the winter but there is also a resident population. It became highly endangered in the 1960s and early 1970s but has staged a comeback since the use of DDT as a pesticide was banned.

K-36 nos 486 (BLW 58587/1925) and 482 (BLW 58541/1925) stand outside Durango roundhouse in the evening of 23 September 2011. The railway has four K-36s, nos 480-2 and 486, and they handle most of its trains. Two K-28s, nos 473 and 476, are also currently in use as well as no 493, one of the ten K-37 class 2-8-2s which were rebuilt from standard gauge 2-8-0s between 1928 and 1930, and were the most powerful locos on the Rio Grande's narrow gauge.

No 478 stands on the turntable at Durango on 23 September 2011. Nos 486 and 482 are to the right. The railway's current owners, Allen Harper, a Florida real estate developer, and his wife Carol, took over from Mr Bradshaw in 1998, and most years they run an evening event in the autumn when photographers are welcomed at Durango roundhouse. No 478 was set aside in 2016 and since then has been a static exhibit at a small museum in part of the roundhouse. There is no current plan for her to return to service.

The Rio Grande's C-19 class 2-8-0 no 346 (Baldwin 5712/1881), originally numbered 406 and named CUMBRES, has always been one of the most prized exhibits at the Colorado Railroad Museum at Golden, near Denver. She was one of eleven locos in the class, all of which were built in 1881.  More than 150 2-8-0s were built for the Rio Grande in the late 1870s and 1880s when many new lines were being constructed, and were the workhorses on the Antonito-Durango and other mountain routes for many years until the K-27s arrived. Three years after being withdrawn in 1947 no 346 was bought for preservation by Robert W Richardson, who went on to found the museum, hence the appearance of his name on her cabside. She is now the oldest working loco in Colorado. The loco was one of three which were on loan to the Colorado & Southern RR in the 1930s, and while there she was severely damaged in a runaway on the Kenosha Pass. A repair was carried out in only three weeks at the Chicago Burlington & Quincy RR's shops at Denver, and she still carries the steel cab and a one-piece boiler jacket without any bands with which she was fitted then. Here she stands beside the museum's loco shed on 25 September 2011. The boiler jackets on many Rio Grande locos were painted green until about the 1930s. Two other class members are preserved at the Knott's Berry park.

This 2-8-0 began life as the Denver, South Park and Pacific RR's no 51 (Baldwin 4919/1880). The railway was later reorganised as the Denver Leadville & Gunnison RR and she became their no 191. The DL&G went on to become a subsidiary of the Union Pacific. The loco is the oldest surviving one to have spent her working life in Colorado. She is now a static exhibit at the Golden museum, where I saw her on 25 September 2011.

The preserved section of the 3ft gauge Sumpter Valley Railway runs for about five miles through the broad Powder River valley between Sumpter and McEwen, in northeastern Oregon. It's before dawn on 1 February 2014, and the preservation society's two steam locos are both in action. On the left WH Eccles 0-4-4-0 no 3 (Heisler 1306/1915) is already attached to her train, while 2-8-2 no 19 (Alco 61980/1920) has just emerged from the engine shed at McEwen. She and her sister no 20 were the last steam locos to be supplied new to the railway.

The SVR was built in stages westwards from its junction with the Union Pacific at Baker City. It opened to McEwen, twenty two miles away, in 1891 and services were extended to Sumpter five years later. The Eccles company ran one of the many logging branches off its mainline, and their locos frequently operated over its metals. Here no 3 catches the dawn sunshine at McEwen on 2 February 2014. The unusually-shaped tank wagon came from the West Side Lumber Co's 3ft gauge railway, which was based at Tuolumne, in northern California, and was the last narrow gauge logging line to operate in the state.

Virtually all the old SVR closed in 1947 and was dismantled, leaving just a mile or so of line at Baker City which lasted for a few more years. In 1971 a group of volunteers set out to rebuild the Sumpter-McEwen section, and the first part reopened in 1976 with no 3 as the working loco. Here no 19 makes an all-out effort as she heads through McEwen station early in the morning of 2 February 2014.

The valley was comprehensively dredged for gold in the early 1900s and has been almost barren ever since. On 1 February 2014 no 19 heads for Sumpter and takes her freight train past one of the many troughs left over from the dredging, with the Elkhorn Mountains as a backdrop.

No 19 works hard midway between McEwen and Sumpter on 1 February 2014. She and no 20 were sold in 1940 to the White Pass line. They had become surplus after being replaced by two large Mallet tank locos which came second-hand from the Uintah Railway in Utah and Colorado. The SVR converted the Mallets to tender locos and kept the tenders from nos 19 and 20 to run with them. In 1947 the Mallets and the tenders were sold to the International Railways of Central America for operation in Guatemala. The locos were scrapped many years later but the tenders survived, as did nos 19 and 20. Eventually the two 2-8-2s and the two tenders all returned to be reunited at the SVR, and no 19 first ran again in 1996.

On 2 February 2014 no 3 stands in the loop midway along the line as no 19 takes her train towards McEwen.

Near Sumpter the line runs through the pine forests typical of eastern Oregon and here no 19 runs through the trees on 2 February 2014.

The afternoon of 1 February 2014 was cloudy, but a momentary break in the cloud produced a spectacular sunset as no 19 waited at McEwen.

For many years Laws was the northern terminus of the old 3ft gauge Owens Valley line, originally the southern part of the Carson & Colorado Railway whose first section south from Mound House, near Carson City, opened in 1880. Three years later it reached Keeler, 300 miles away. The C&C was taken over by Southern Pacific in 1900, after which some parts were converted to standard gauge and others closed. Passenger traffic ended as long ago as 1938, the cue for Ward and Betty Kimball to buy their SP carriage from the line, and the section north of Laws was closed completely. The last freight train between Laws and Keeler ran in 1960. At the time of the closure SP made a gift to the local authority of Laws station, many wagons and 4-6-0 no 9, to enable them to set up the museum. They also presented no 18 (Baldwin 37395/1918) to the local authority at Independence, further south along the old line, where she became an exhibit at the Eastern California Museum. Much more recently no 18 was restored to working order by a committed group of enthusiasts at Independence. Here she takes her train away from Laws station on 23 September 2017, while making her first visit there after her restoration was completed.

The 3ft gauge Death Valley RR, to the southeast of the Owens Valley, was built in 1914 to serve borax mines near Furnace Creek. It was served by two 2-8-0s, one of which is preserved there. The railway was highly scenic, dropping from an altitude of 2,041ft at Death Valley Junction to 190ft below sea level at Furnace Creek. The borax was running out in 1928, and the line bought this JG Brill railcar in an unsuccessful attempt to boost tourist traffic. It closed three years later and all the rail and stock were removed for construction and use on the new United States Potash Railroad, serving phosphate mines near Loving, in New Mexico. When this line closed in 1967 the Laws museum rescued the railcar as well as a caboose and some wagons. Much more recently the railcar has been restored to working order and here it waits for access to the running line at Laws as no 18 goes past on 23 September 2017. Despite carrying the number 5 it was the Death Valley's only railcar. It bears more than a passing resemblance to no M-1 at the East Broad Top with its JG Brill parts.

Nos 9 (Baldwin 34095/1909) and 18 were two of three 4-6-0s acquired by SP when it took over the Nevada-California-Oregon Railway in 1927, the third being no 8 which is now preserved at Sparks in northern Nevada, once the home of a major SP loco repair facility. Their distinctive round-topped tenders show that they were oil-burners. It's dusk at Laws on 22 September 2017, and no 18 stands in the station, with the light from her headlight reflecting off no 9 in the foreground.

The West Side Lumber Co's railway at Tuolumne operated between 1898 and 1962. Other than two early 0-4-0STs its motive power consisted of four Heislers and nine Shays, and several examples of both types have survived. Three-truck Shay no 12 (Lima 3302/1927) has been an exhibit at the museum at Golden for several years and I saw her there on 25 September 2011. No 40 (Baldwin 53777/1920), whose tender can be seen on the left, was one of many 2-8-0s which worked for IRCA in Guatemala and El Salvador. She was purchased for preservation, along with 2-8-0 no 111 in 1972, while residing at San Salvador engine shed, which appears to have been her home for most of her life before preservation. After the purchase they travelled by rail right across El Salvador and Guatemala to the Mexican border, with no 40 hauling the train for much of the way, and completed their journey to the US on wagons in a NdeM standard gauge train. Both nos 40 and 111 now run on the Georgetown Loop RR, up in the Rocky Mountains to the west of Golden.

The 3ft gauge Eureka & Palisade RR's no 4 EUREKA (Baldwin 3763/1875) was supplied shortly before the opening of this 85-mile line in north eastern Nevada on 22 October 1875. In 1896 she moved to a logging railway at Hobart Mills in California, and stayed there until it closed in December 1937. She was sold for scrap, but was rescued by Warner Bros in 1939 and became a Hollywood star. Her last movie was *The Shootist* in 1976, co-starring John Wayne who was also making his farewell appearance. In the 1870s many US locos were finished in highly elaborate paint schemes, and EUREKA was no exception. At Hollywood she still carried her original paint under many later layers. In 1978 the California State Railroad Museum at Sacramento was in the process of restoring a similar 4-4-0, no 12 SONOMA of the North Pacific Coast RR (Baldwin 3843/1876), and obtained permission to strip off the newer paint from EUREKA to record and copy the original. EUREKA moved from Hollywood to an amusement park near Las Vegas, but was badly damaged by fire in 1986, and might well have been scrapped were it not for Dan Markoff, a Las Vegas railfan. Well aware of her historical importance he bought her, took her home and set about restoring her to working order. All her paint had gone, but thanks to the Californian museum's work he was able to recreate her original livery. Now restored to her original condition, she shows off her magnificent livery on 15 December 2018 while visiting the Boulder City branch of the Nevada State Railroad Museum, not far from Las Vegas.

EUREKA simmers after finishing her day's work at the Boulder City museum in the early evening of 15 December 2018. The loco generally visits the museum every year for a few weeks before Christmas and runs at weekends while she is there.

3ft gauge 2-6-0 GLENBROOK (Baldwin 3712/1875) is just a few weeks older than EUREKA, and was another loco to benefit from the work done by the Californian museum in 1978. Wendell Huffman is the Curator of History at the Carson City branch of the Nevada museum, and kindly pulled her out into the morning sunshine on 24 September 2017 so that friends and I could take her photo. She was built for a forestry railway close to Lake Tahoe, which straddles the state border between California and Nevada, and moved in about 1899 to a new line serving Tahoe City. In 1937 she was sold on to the Nevada County Narrow Gauge RR, but only as a source of spares, and was soon stripped down. The loco has only survived thanks to Miss Hope Bliss, her original owner's daughter. She bought her in 1942 after the Nevada County line closed and presented her to the predecessor of the Nevada museum, and many of her missing parts followed her there. The loco has recently been restored to working order.

The 3ft gauge White Pass & Yukon's 2-8-2 no 73 (Baldwin 73352/1947) stands outside Skagway station in Alaska before setting off with a tourist train for Fraser, British Columbia, on 13 June 2011. Four of these 2-8-2s were built between 1938 and 1947. They were the last new steam locos to be bought by the railway, though many others were brought in to the line by the US army during the Second World War. The line headed inland for 118 miles from Skagway to Whitehorse, now the capital of the Yukon, and was built in the aftermath of the Klondike goldrush which began in July 1897. So many stampeders headed north that a railway through the mountains became an attractive economic proposition despite the heavy engineering involved. The first train on a short section out of Skagway ran in 1898, and the railway was completed through to Whitehorse in 1900. The stampeders' onward journey down the Yukon River to the Klondike district was relatively straightforward. Many of the White Pass's coaches predate the opening and came secondhand from railways in the Lower 48, as Alaskans like to call the continental US.

The railway is dwarfed by the mountains at the White Pass. No 73 has completed the twenty-mile climb from the coast at Skagway and has just crossed from Alaska into British Columbia on 13 June 2011. She is about to pass a train which is standing in the loop beside the frozen Summit Lake, at an altitude of 874m. It is being hauled by one of eleven General Electric GEX3341-pattern diesel-electric locos supplied to the railway between 1954 and 1966, now venerable machines in their own right. The lake forms a part of the headwaters of the Yukon River.

2-8-0 no 69 (Baldwin 32962/1908) was the White Pass's other working steam loco when I visited in 2011. Here she takes an enthusiasts' special train out of Fraser station in British Columbia on 11 June 2011. Traffic on the line fell away in the early 1900s as the Klondike goldrush subsided, and no 69 was the last loco to be supplied to it for many years until the arrival of the 2-8-2s. She was withdrawn in 1954, and sold two years later to a tourist railway in the Lower 48. In 2001 the White Pass bought her back and returned her to service in 2008.

No 69 runs through the Skagway River gorge on 11 June 2011 near the end of her journey from Fraser.

No 69 heads a short demonstration freight train near Fraser on 12 June 2011.

The same train runs through the bleak countryside near the summit on 12 June 2011. Sadly no 69 has been set aside since 2013 in need of further overhaul and most of the wagons in this train have also now been taken out of traffic.

The Tanana Valley RR's 0-4-0ST no 1 (Porter 1972/1899) stands outside her shed at Fairbanks, Alaska. Few locos can deserve to carry the number 1 more than this little 3ft gauge machine. She arrived in the Klondike district during the goldrush years and was the first loco to work in the Yukon. In 1903 she moved to the new Tanana Valley line at Fairbanks, and became the first to work in the interior of Alaska. In 1917 the US government bought the Tanana Valley to use its route into the town for the standard gauge Alaska RR, which continued to operate part of the narrow gauge until 1930 as its Chatanika branch. The little loco then ran as their no 1. She was withdrawn in 1922 and was preserved on account of her role in Alaska's history. The Friends of the Tanana Valley Railroad was formed to restore her in 1992, and she now makes occasional outings over a circle of track at Fairbanks. They very kindly steamed her for me on 8 June 2011. It would have been a bright sunny evening but for a forest fire whose smoke had penetrated the upper atmosphere. These fires are not uncommon in the district where summer temperatures can be surprisingly warm for a place which is so far north.

No 1 crosses a stream during the course of her journey at Fairbanks on 8 June 2011. The railway's volunteers invited me to drive her – an unexpected treat! A great little railway and one that's well worth visiting despite its remote location.

The Tanana Valley only ever owned a few locos. The government added two more, a second-hand 2-8-0 and then 4-6-0 no 152 (Baldwin 53296/1920) which was built new for the line. After the closure no 152 went into store until becoming one of the locos to serve the US army on the White Pass & Yukon during the Second World War. After peace returned she was sent for scrap at Seattle, but was rescued and eventually found a home at the Huckleberry RR. Here she runs alongside the frozen CS Mott Lake, a reservoir serving Flint, on the very cold morning of 15 January 2019. Michigan is far enough north for silhouette views to be feasible even at midday in winter. The leading coach, no 40 of the Ferrocarriles Unidos de Yucatán in south eastern México, was probably built in the 1880s. It is one of many historic vehicles in the Huckleberry's collection. On the right is 2-8-0 no 4 (Baldwin 24306/1904) of the FC Potosi y Rio Verde in northern México. It may look as though she was also in steam, but this was just an illusion and she hasn't run for many years.

It's almost sunset as no 152 makes her way along the Huckleberry line on 15 January 2019. After several years out of use she was restored to working order in 2018, and carries an approximation of her original green colour scheme.

Many Mexican locos were destroyed during a devastating civil war between 1910 and 1920. To make good the losses on the narrow gauge twenty of these G-030 class 2-8-0s were built in 1921, and a further eight in 1924. The short, stubby chimneys and the large, centrally mounted headlights were trademarks of NdeM's narrow gauge locos. 2-8-0 no 279 (Baldwin 55110/1921) stands in Cuautla engine shed on 18 November 2012, with some of NdeM's characteristic boxy second class carriages on the left. The loco should have been operating and she was duly lit up but then local political considerations led to her outing being cancelled at the last minute. She was still warm, but definitely not in steam. Sadly parts were stolen from her after her boiler certificate expired in 2013 and there are currently no plans to restore her. The old loco enjoys a measure of popularity amongst México's population. She has even appeared on one of the country's banknotes!

The line north from Cuautla to a summit at Amecameca and on to Los Reyes, a part of the later route to México City, was opened as the FC Morelos in 1881, and was one of the earliest of México's many 3ft gauge railways. The section between Cuautla and Yecapiztla was kept in situ after it closed in 1973. It reopened as a heritage railway in 1986 with no 279 as its working steam loco, but by the time I visited the line had been cut back to just a few hundred metres at Cuautla station. Gerald M Best's book *Central American Holiday* was published back in 1963 as a holiday guide, but such is the dearth of published histories of railways in this part of the world that it is still an essential reference book. A striking photo of a double-headed train crossing this viaduct at Nepantla, near Amacameca, appears on its cover. The viaduct is close to the birthplace of Sor Juana Inés de la Cruz, a seventeenth century writer, poet and nun who is much respected in México, and is now surrounded by a cultural centre dedicated to her memory. Here NdeM 286 (Baldwin 57926/1924) stands at its far end. She was damaged while spending time in NdeM's Huehuetoca scrapyard and perhaps looked her best at a distance on 18 November 2012, but more recently she has been taken in hand and now looks magnificent.

Guatemala's first railway opened in 1880, and was extended to Guatemala City in 1884. The fine central terminus station there became the hub of the 3ft gauge IRCA, which was formed by the merger of several local lines in Guatemala and El Salvador in 1912. Trains left for Guatemala's Atlantic and Pacific coasts, for its Mexican border where they connected with a NdeM standard gauge branch, and for the extensive system in El Salvador. All this has gone, but the station houses an attractive museum of the old railway. No 205 (Baldwin 74135/1948) was one of the last of a series of generally similar 2-8-2s which had been built since 1930, and I saw her there on 14 April 2012.

2-8-0 no 34 (Baldwin 15337/1897) started life as the FC de Central Salvador's no 2, and later moved to the FFCC de Guatemala; both lines were IRCA constituents. She is now another resident at the museum. 14 April 2012.

2-8-2 no 204 (Baldwin 74135/1948) stands at the entrance to the station on 14 April 2012. Services in Guatemala became erratic after IRCA's lines there were nationalised in 1968, and came to a complete standstill in 1996. Things looked up in 1997 when operations were taken over by a company run by Henry Posner III, a US railroad entrepreneur and enthusiast. No 204 worked several enthusiast excursions in the first part of the 2000s and her last outing appears to have been in 2006. Disputes with the government came to a head in 2007 and led to a suspension of services once more. It took several years of litigation before the Guatemalan government paid compensation to Mr Posner's company, and by then the widespread theft of rail and of steel from many of the splendid viaducts along the line had rendered the railway unusable. Amongst his other railway interests Mr Posner has gone on to become one of the professional railwaymen involved in the rescue of the East Broad Top.

Zacapa was an important junction, where the international line to El Salvador left the mainline from Guatemala City to the Atlantic coast. Sadly this scene of dilapidation at the engine shed there on 15 April 2012 is typical of how things now are on what remains of Guatemala's railways. No 153 (Baldwin 60589/1928) was one of the earliest of the standard 2-8-2s. Partially visible in front of her is 2-8-2 no 183 (Baldwin 73098/1947), and to the right inside the engine shed there's a glimpse of 2-8-2 no 199 (Baldwin 74129/1948). The Cia Agricola lettering on no 153's tender refers to one of United Fruit's trading entities in Guatemala. The company was heavily dependent on IRCA to convey bananas from its plantations to the Atlantic coast for shipment to the US and elsewhere, and for much of its existence the railway was effectively a United Fruit subsidiary.

A much happier scene at San Salvador engine shed awaited me on 13 April 2012. IRCA's railways in El Salvador were nationalised in 1974, and in the following year they were merged with the older FC de El Salvador which had been state-owned since 1962. The combined system became known as Fenadesal. When I arrived the shed staff were raising steam in Fenadesal 2-8-0 no 12 (Baldwin 58224/1925) for my benefit, even though she was supposed to be unserviceable. What kind people! The loco was formerly IRCA no 102. Next to her is sister loco no 101 (Baldwin 58441/1925).

Later on 13 April 2012 no 12 has steam up and has ventured outside San Salvador engine shed. Sadly the railway closed four months later when the track on the line to Apopa, the only one which still saw passenger traffic, was found to have become unsafe. It had previously ceased operation between 2002 and 2007 but this time the closure looks set to be permanent. In 2015 a museum was set up in the shed and the adjoining workshops, with nos 12 and 101 as the principal exhibits. It was a real privilege to be given this last little taste of what a magnificent railway IRCA must have been in its prime.

In the late 1930s United Fruit ordered a series of 2-8-2s from Krupp in Germany to work its new 3ft 6ins gauge FC del Sur in southern Costa Rica. Other than the gauge they would have been similar to locos which Krupp had just built for IRCA which were close copies of its Baldwin 2-8-2s. In the event Krupp could not complete the order because of the Second World War and United Fruit turned instead to Baldwin, which supplied six of these 2-8-2s between 1940 and 1946. The line ran through one of the wettest districts anywhere in the Americas and was subject to severe flooding. Diesels arrived in 1951 but couldn't cope with the floods, and three of the Baldwins stayed on to help. 2-8-2 no 84 (Baldwin 72669/1946) stands at Palmar Sur, the railway's inland terminus on the Río Térraba close to Costa Rica's Pacific coast, in the early morning of 16 April 2012. In the foreground is one of several stone spheres found in the district. They are almost certainly pre-Columbian artefacts, but their origin and purpose are a mystery. Just visible to the right is a tank car, one of many pieces of equipment built for the US authorities towards the end of the Second World War when they expected to have to resuscitate Japan's railways after peace returned, but in the event the system survived largely intact and the US equipment wasn't needed.

The FC del Sur was built to serve new banana plantations around Palmar Sur, to which United Fruit was relocating after older plantations in Honduras and Panama, and near Costa Rica's Caribbean coast, had been ravaged by crop disease. The new railway took the bananas to the magnificent natural harbour at Golfito, 85km away, and there was another long line which connected with the Chiriquí 3ft system over the border in Panama. In later years branches were built to serve more plantations being established along the route and by the mid-1950s there were 315km of track. The concession to build the railway required that it should be a public carrier with passenger services, and it was equipped with full overhaul facilities because of its remote location. It closed in 1984 when the Pacific plantations also succumbed to the disease, though by then the concession only had four years left to run. 2-8-2 no 82 (Baldwin 62445/1940) and her train were run into a shed at Golfito on the closure and left in case their services were needed again. They were still there on 16 April 2012.

Regular steam working on the 3ft gauge Ferrocarriles Nacionales de Colombia, the country's state railways, ended in the 1970's, but returned in 1982 when Dr Eduardo Rodriguez, its assistant general manager, oversaw the repair of several locos for a tourist service out of Bogotá. It made use of luxury coaches laying over during the weekend between trips down to Santa Marta on the Caribbean coast. The trains were much loved within the city, but their future looked bleak when the state railways closed in 1992. Dr Rodriguez and colleagues purchased the coaches and several locos in 1993 and restarted the service. FNC no 2-8-2 no 72 (Baldwin 73056/1947) awaits her next turn of duty at Bogotá engine shed on 10 December 2011. She was built for the FC de Antioquia where she carried the same number. To the left is 2-8-2 no 85 (Baldwin 73051/1947), originally Antioquia no 73, and, just visible above no 85's tender, is 4-8-0 no 76 (Baldwin 73095/1947) which was about to leave before taking a train to La Caro.

No 76 sets off from Bogotá engine shed on 10 December 2011. The loco started out life as no 10 of the FC Ambalema-Imbagué, a line which was only 65km long and was run by the Department of Tolima, one of the country's principal coffee-growing regions, until being taken over by the state railway in 1953. These 4-8-0s were designed back in 1924 by PC Dewhurst, the state railway's talented chief engineer. The leading wheels are flangeless, and the rear axle incorporates Cartazzi slides. These features, and their high adhesive factor of 85%, made the locos especially suitable for the country's twisty and steeply-graded railways, and they were nicknamed *the snakes* by Colombia's enginemen. Mr Dewhurst moved away in 1929 and orders for his 4-8-0s ceased. The Ambalema line had few sharp curves and wasn't very hilly, but had used the 4-8-0 design since 1928. When it needed new locos in 1947 it ordered two more, nos 9 and 10. Altogether no fewer than 108 served Colombia's railways.

No 76 backs into the Estación de la Sabana at Bogotá on 10 December 2011. The loco on the right is 2-8-2 no 44 (Baldwin 60008/1927), a lighter loco from the Antioquia where she ran under the same number. She has been stored at Bogotá for many years for possible future restoration. The current station building, a magnificent neo-classical structure, dates from 1917 and was designed by William Lidstone, a British engineer. It replaced an earlier building erected when the railway between Bogotá and Facatativá, 40km to the northwest, was built between 1882 and 1889. In later years the Estación de la Sabana became the central station for all the railways serving Bogotá.

The tourist service, marketed as Turistren since its rescue in 1993, now operates every Sunday throughout the year. Its trains mostly run to Zipaquirá, an attractive old Spanish colonial town. The line to Zipaquirá leaves the one to Facatativá in the northwestern outskirts of Bogotá and runs through the city's sprawling suburbs before reaching the open valley of the Río Bogotá. It was built between 1889 and 1898 and was extended northwards from 1905 as part of project to build a line to the Caribbean coast, though it never went much further and when a route through to the coast was eventually completed in the early 1950s it took the form of an extension of the existing line through Facatativá and down to the valley of the Rio Magdalena at La Dorada. Here no 76 heads towards La Caro on 10 December 2011. This train had been chartered by a Bogotá bank for a Christmas staff outing to a country club next to the line near La Caro.

The train laid over at La Caro for much of the day, and just before sunset was setting off to collect its passengers and return to Bogotá on 10 December 2011. All the railways to the north and west of the city were originally metre gauge. The Facatativá line was converted to 3ft as early as 1925 but the Zipaquirá one wasn't tackled until 1953, as part of a final drive to unify the gauge of the country's railways which was completed four years later.

The 2ft 6ins gauge railway at São João del Rei, a beautiful old Portuguese colonial city in Brazil's Minas Gerais state, was built by the Estrada de Ferro Oeste de Minas. At its greatest extent the line was no less than 602km long, and branches made it longer still. The length had shrunk to 202km by the time commercial operation finished in 1983, because much of the route further west and north had been converted to metre gauge. Happily heritage trains still run on the 12.8km section between São João del Rei and Tiradentes and, like Turistren, this is a year-round operation.  4-6-0 no 41 (Baldwin 38011/1912) has been restored in nearly all respects to her OdeM condition including her wooden pilot. The locos were given new numbers at some date after 1920, most probably as part of a more general renumbering by the Rede Mineira de Viação, a railway formed in 1931 by the merger of several lines in Minas Gerais including the OdeM. All the São João del Rei locos carry the later numbers and no 41 was previously OdeM no 43. Here she peeps out from under the splendid overall roof at São João del Rei station before departing for Tiradentes on 24 August 2012.

Later in the morning of 24 August 2012 no 41 and her well-filled train approach Tiradentes. The first part of the railway west from its junction with the EF Central do Brasil at Sitio, later called Antônio Carlos, as far as Barroso opened in 1880, and the section on through Tiradentes to São João del Rei was completed in the following year.

The sun glints off the polished brass on no 41's firebox as she stands at Tiradentes station on 24 August 2012. For many years the line's principal traffic was limestone from quarries west of São João del Rei to a cement factory at Barroso and it was the factory's closure in 1983 which led to the abandonment of most of the railway.

2-8-0 no 68 (Baldwin 52256/1919) rests outside São João del Rei engine shed on 23 August 2012, painted in the RMV's paintscheme. She is the line's youngest surviving loco.  When I first visited the railway in 1977 she was even more brightly painted with many parts picked out in yellow. She is now comparatively sober, though the trees beneath which she is standing are doing their best to provide some yellow instead!

The roundhouse or rotunda at São João del Rei is just what its title describes, a 360 degrees round building. It contains no fewer than twenty two bays plus two through roads, and the turntable in the middle is open to the elements. It burned down in 1972 but was rebuilt early in the 1980s. Happily one of the cast iron columns, made in Glasgow, survived the fire and was used as a pattern for the replacements. Seven little Baldwin locos stand inside on 23 August 2012. Nos 37 and 38 (37082-3/1911), 40 (38010/1911) and 43 (38051/1912) are 4-6-0's. Nos 55 (12934/1892) and 62 (13831/1893) were members of a series of twelve 2-8-0s which began life between 1892 and 1894 as Vauclain compounds, and were later rebuilt as simples, while no 69 (14134/1894) seems always to have been a simple. There are also three metre gauge RMV steam locos there. The RFFSA, Brazil's nationalised railway, set up the heritage operation when the remainder of the line was closed. By far the principal business on the railways in Minas Gerais is the bulk haulage of minerals to the coast for shipment and it must be highly profitable. RFFSA's system has since been privatised, but happily the concession for the Minas Gerais lines requires that this heritage service, and the museum which now occupies the roundhouse, must be maintained. Just outside the roundhouse, and built on former railway land, stands the excellent Pousada Rotunda. There's no need to translate this name into English!

2-8-0 no 60 (Baldwin 13832/1893) is another former Vauclain compound. Here she stands under the roof at São João del Rei station on 23 August 2012. She's one of several more locos, and other pieces of equipment, which are now on display at the station as a part of the museum.

The old RMV line running north from Cruzeiro to Três Corações, 170km away, originally the British-owned Rio and Minas Railway, closed in 1991. The Sul de Minas chapter of the Associação Brasileira de Preservação Ferroviária, Brazil's main preservation society, looks after 90kms of it and operates trains over two sections, each about 10kms long. This is the more southerly one, based at Passa Quatro. There's a steep climb between Manacá and Coronel Fulgêncio, at the northern end of a long tunnel under the Serra da Mantiquera which forms the border between Minas Gerais and São Paulo states. The tunnel was the scene of fighting in 1932 when São Paulo state embarked upon armed insurrection against the dictatorship of Getúlio Vargas, who had overthrown Brazil's federal constitution and seized power two years previously. There are still bullet holes in Coronel Fulgêncio's station building. The OdeM went on to build a large metre gauge system. Its Pacific no 164 (Baldwin 58552/1925), later RMV no 332, crosses Rua Cruzeiro as she approaches Manacá on 19 August 2012, on her way from Passa Quatro to Coronel Fulgêncio. She is hauling a wooden coach, one of six built for the EF Central do Brasil in Belo Horizonte in 1956 which were rescued by ABPF in 1999. This section of the railway dates from 1884, and the heritage operation began in 2004. No 332 is the only loco to have travelled in preservation all the way from Cruzeiro, through the tunnel, as far as Passa Quatro.

The metre gauge EF Mogiana was promoted by coffee farmers in São Paulo state, and at its greatest extent in the 1920s it operated almost 2,000km of route in the east of the state and the west of Minas Gerais. The railway between Campinas and Jaguariúna, 38km away, opened in 1875 and was the earliest section of its mainline. South from Campinas coffee for export was transported by the Brazilian-owned Companhia Paulista's 5ft 3ins gauge line as far as Jundiai, and on from there to the coast by the British-owned 5ft 3ins gauge São Paulo Railway. The Campinas to Jaguariúna section was replaced by a mixed gauge railway on a different alignment and closed in 1977. The part north of Anhumas, in the outskirts of Campinas, became the first line to be preserved by ABPF, thanks to the generosity of FEPASA, then São Paulo state's railway authority. It is 24km long and reopened in 1984. On 25 August 2012 RMV 2-8-2 no 505 (Schwartzkopff 8904/1927) approaches a level crossing near Carlos Gomes on her way north from Anhumas. The depot at Carlos Gomes is still home to most of ABPF's steam locos and carriages even though the association now operates several heritage railways throughout much of the country.

No 505 has steam to spare after arriving at Jaguariúna on 25 August 2012. The railway through the town was rebuilt on a new alignment in 1945, and the magnificent station building constructed by the Mogiana dates from then. A small part of it be seen on the right. Much more recently the road in the foreground was built, occupying what was previously the site of an island platform. No 505 ran for the Rede Sul Mineira de Viação as their no 314 until the 1931 merger which created the RMV. She was one of a group of fifteen 2-8-2s and fourteen Pacifics which were ordered by the Minas Gerais government from Schwartzkopff for the RSM and the OdeM between 1925 and 1927. Another of the group, RMV Pacific no 307, formerly RSM no 268, is one of the metre gauge locos in the roundhouse at São João del Rei. No 505 was physically rescued by Patrick Dollinger, ABPF's founder, in the nick of time when he was found a scrapman lighting up his torch at Barra Mansa, and persuaded him to extinguish it. She is one of no fewer than twelve former RMV locos which Julio Moraes, ABPF's director of patrimony in its early years, was able to persuade RFFSA to present to them, another brilliant act of generosity.

Apart from no 505 the other eleven locos given to ABPF were ex-RMV 4-6-0s nos 205, 210, 215, 232, 235 and 236, Pacifics nos 332 and 338, 2-8-0 no 431 and 2-8-2s nos 520 and 522. They were lying at Divinópolis, Ribeirão Vermelho and Barra Mansa, and the story of many people's endeavours to rescue them all and to transport them by rail to safety would fill an entire book! RMV no 215 (Baldwin 37710/1912), originally OdeM no 110, was still in service as the shunter at the old RMV's works at Ribeirão Vermelho at the time the twelve locos were presented to ABPF and became the first to run on the Anhumas to Jaguariúna line in preservation. The emphasis on preserving RMV locos arose because steam operation was only just ending on the Viação Férrea Centro Oeste, its nationalised successor, or RFFSA SR2 as it was later more prosaically called, whereas in São Paulo state the withdrawal of steam was more or less complete. Very sadly Patrick Dollinger died in 1986 following a horrific road accident in the US and no 215 now carries his name out of respect for his pioneering work in Brazilian preservation. Here the loco takes water in the yard at Anhumas on 9th July 2013. Altogether Baldwin built thirty seven of these 4-6-0s for the OdeM between 1910 and 1920, and no fewer than thirteen have been preserved. Two of them, RMV nos 220 and 239, are at the São João del Rei roundhouse.

The Paulista's 5ft 3ins gauge mainline ended at Bauru, more than 300km northwest of Jundiai, and metre gauge feeder lines went even further inland. Its venerable metre gauge 4-6-0 no 604 (Baldwin 14255/1895) worked for many years on secondary routes out of São Carlos, a junction on the mainline 162km north of Campinas, until being withdrawn in the 1960s. She was on station pilot duty at Anhumas on 9 July 2013 and carries the olive green paintscheme used by the Paulista for many years.

EF Noroeste do Brasil Pacific no 401 (Baldwin 53766/1920), painted in the railway's characteristic green livery, leaves Anhumas station for Jaguariúna on 9 July 2013. The first section of the NOB opened to the northwest from Bauru in 1906. By 1937 construction had progressed as far as Andradina, in the far west of São Paulo state. From there it headed across Mato Grosso do Sul through the vast marshy Pantanal, one of the world's great wildlife habitats and also inhabited by diminishing numbers of pre-Columbian peoples who used to attack trains with bows and arrows during the line's early years. In 1952 it reached Corumbá, more than 1,000km away from Bauru, and now joins the Bolivian railways there. It became a part of RFFSA when the state railway was formed five years later. The leading wooden coach with its high domed roof and arched windows is one of a series built for it in the late 1940s and early 1950s in readiness for the opening to Corumbá. Passenger services ended in 1995, shortly before RFFSA was broken up and privatised – a sad end to what must have been a magnificent train ride. One result was that many of these distinctive coaches became available for preservation, and they now grace several of Brazil's heritage railways. No fewer than three other NOB locos are preserved at Bauru's railway museum, including 2-6-0 no 278 which is usually in working order.

Amongst British enthusiasts the Mogiana is well known for the forty seven 4-6-0s, with their distinctive angled running boards, built for it by Beyer Peacock between 1891 and 1912. Some were two-cylinder compounds, though no 417 (works no 3819/1896) at the Hotel Fazenda Duas Marias, out in the countryside near Jaguariúna, is a simple. She is attached to three wooden metre gauge coaches, complete with their old furnishings and fittings which now form a part of the hotel's restaurant. The markings on the floor plates of their end platforms and elsewhere suggest that there are one each from the EF Bragantina, the EF Sorocabana and the Paulista. The building in which they stand looks as though it was built by the Mogiana, down to the shade of yellow ochre in which they painted their stations, and the distinctive shape of the windows and their surrounds which are much like those at Jaguariúna. I do not believe that there has ever been any railway there but have not found out if this is a relocated building or a replica. Six of these Mogiana 4-6-0s have been preserved, including two of the compounds which are awaiting restoration at Carlos Gomes. The sharp-eyed will see that no 417 is missing her tender, and also her chimney cap, but all the same I thought this was a delightful scene. 25 August 2012.

The São Paulo Railway ran from Jundiai, through Luz station in the centre of São Paulo city, and reached the sea at Santos. For many years it was hugely profitable since it had a de facto monopoly in the transport of coffee destined for export from much of São Paulo state. In the early twentieth century the Mogiana threatened its monopoly by planning a new route from the Campinas district to the sea. It would have passed through the territory served by the Bragantina, another metre gauge coffee line, which dated from 1887 and connected Bragança Paulista with the SPR's mainline at Campo Lipo Paulista, near Jundiai. In order to see off the threat the SPR bought the Bragantina in 1903 and it became their only non-5ft 3ins section. Much later they provided it with no 18 (Beyer Peacock 6860/1937), its newest loco. Two similar 4-6-0s had run on the line since 1911, very much like the ones on the Mogiana, and no 18 was perhaps the last development of the type. The Bragantina closed in 1967 and she was acquired for preservation by the Museu de Arqueologia Industrial Thomaz Cruz at Mairiporã, near São Paulo city, Brazil's first privately-run railway preservation venture. She is still in working order and is usually steamed once a year for a festival in October. I saw her at the museum on 22 August 2012. An early Paulista wooden coach stands on the right.

The other section of the old RMV metre gauge line north from Cruzeiro which the Sul de Minas chapter of ABPF now operates is based at São Lourenço, where Central do Brasil 2-8-2 no 1424 (Alco 59712/1927) waits to set off for Soledade de Minas on 26 August 2012. The first heritage train here ran in 2000. The Central was one of Brazil's largest railways, with 5ft 3ins gauge mainlines from Rio de Janeiro to São Paulo city and to Belo Horizonte, and many secondary metre gauge routes. No 1424 was one of a class of thirteen which at first were all based at Sete Lagoas engine shed, north of Belo Horizonte. She went on to work the last steam train on the old Central system in 1973. The Central used to maintain separate number series for its 5ft 3ins and metre gauge locos. In 1930 it added 1000 to the numbers of all its metre gauge locos to put an end to the obvious confusion which this caused.

No 1424 whistles as she approaches Parada Ramon, on her way from São Lourenço to Soledade de Minas, on 26 August 2012. Soledade de Minas was once a major junction between the Cruzeiro-Três Corações line and RSM's long east-west route to Sapucaí, where it connected with the Mogiana. After a period of static display RFFSA restored no 1424 to working order in the 1980s for a short-lived heritage operation at Ouro Preto, and she later worked tourist trains in Rio de Janeiro state. In 1997 she was presented to ABPF together with Central 2-8-0 no 1170 and Leopoldina Railway no 327, a beautiful Beyer Peacock Pacific. She has worked on the São Lourenço line since 2010. The wooden coaches in this train were built at the Central's Belo Horizonte workshops in 1956 and were rescued by ABPF in 1999. The two steel ones at the front were built at the Santa Matilde factory in Três Rios, in the north of Rio de Janeiro state. For many years it was one of Brazil's principal railway carriage builders, but as Brazil's railways declined in importance it diversified into both agricultural machinery and, to the joy of many Brazilians, a line of much-loved sports cars. In all 937 cars were built, but sadly the company became bankrupt in 2005.

On 6 July 2013 EF Dona Tereza Cristina 2-8-2 no 153 (Alco 69445/1941) heads south from Tubarão with a coal train, under the supervision of a feathered friend! The first section of the metre gauge EFDTC, in Santa Catarina state in southern Brazil, opened in 1884. By the 1920's it had developed into a substantial system serving the country's principal coalfield. It had been an exclusively coal-carrying line since regular passenger services ended in 1968, until preservationists began to restore some of its steam locos and brought in former NOB carriages to start a heritage operation.

No 153 heads south from Tubarão with her coal train and approaches a level crossing near Jaguaruna on 6 July 2012. When I first visited the line in 1977 the bodies of the coal wagons were made of wood. They still look much the same but I was surprised to find that the planks appear now to be made of brown-coloured plastic. The railway's preservation group has a fine museum and operating centre at Tubarão with a large collection of locos from the steam era on EFDTC and the industry which it serves. They include no 53, formerly NOB no 408, a Pacific from the same batch as no 401 now on the Anhumas to Jaguariúna line. She moved to EFDTC in 1964 and has survived thanks to ending up as a stationary boiler at Tubarão.

EFDTC bought fourteen of these 200 class 2-10-2s second-hand from Argentina in 1980. No 205 (Škoda 1982/1949) stands in Tubarão yard at dawn on 6 July 2013. She was formerly Ferrocarriles Argentinos' no 1352, and was modified at Tubarão by LD Porta, the innovative Argentine engineer, to include his advanced exhaust system - easily recognised by the forward-sloping chimney needed for the blastpipe to clear the superheater header. The fourteen locos made their journey from Argentina by rail in a single long cavalcade, and passed through Bolivia on their way to Brazil. EFDTC has never been connected to the country's metre gauge system and they had to complete their journey to Tubarão by road.

The 600mm gauge EF Perus-Pirapora opened in 1914 between a quarry at Gato Preto and the São Paulo Railway's mainline at Perus. A cement factory built at Perus in 1925 provided most of its business in later years. It also offered a passenger service – informally after 1972 when its owners believed they had withdrawn it, reputedly after taking exception to industrial action at the factory. It closed in 1983, but thanks to preservationists little was scrapped and a heritage operation eventually began over the 4km section between Perus and Corredor. 2-4-2ST no 2 (Alco 66405/1925), one of six similar locos on the old line, takes one of the original coaches through the thick woods of the Parque Anhanguera as she approaches Corredor on 25 August 2012.

The sun has only just risen as Ferrocarriles Argentinos 750mm gauge 2-8-2 no 4 (Baldwin 55432/1922) and her train head through the barren Patagonian countryside near Desvío Thomae on 22 October 2014. The railway runs for no less than 402km between a junction with a broad gauge mainline at Ingeniero Jacobacci, from where the first section opened in 1925, and Esquel which was reached twenty years later. It was part of an ambitious scheme to build a much larger network of 750mm railways intended to encourage settlement in Patagonia. Most of them were never built.

The barren countryside is often almost completely flat and provides a striking contrast with the snow-capped mountains. Here no 4 has crossed a bridge carrying the line over one of the many rivers running off the mountains towards the distant Atlantic Ocean, and heads south towards Mayoco on 22 October 2014. The railway was made famous by Paul Theroux as *The Old Patagonian Express* in his book published in 1979, though local people call it *La Trochita*, which translates loosely as *The Little Narrow Gauge Train*. The enthusiasts who already knew it were joined by increasing numbers of backpackers and adventure tourists, and there was an international outcry when the Argentine state closed it in 1993. It was rescued and reopened as a tourist railway the following year by the governments of the two provinces through which it runs, though generally trains now only operate on some relatively short sections.

Esquel has been an outpost of the Patagonian Welsh community since the late nineteenth century. It lies in the fertile valley of the Rio de los Bandidos, quite a contrast with the arid land elsewhere, and it is easy to see why the Welsh chose to settle there. Here 2-8-2s nos 16 (Baldwin 55544/1924) and 4 head a long mixed train up the hill away from the town on 23 October 2014 and pass apple trees in blossom. Political considerations meant that these twenty five Baldwin locos were needed very quickly and they were all completed in May and June 1922, within forty days after the order for them was placed.

The railway's workshops and operating headquarters are at El Maitén. Just after dawn on 24 October 2014 no 101 (Henschel 19402/1922) was being prepared for an outing. She was the first of fifty 2-8-2s supplied by this builder a few months after the Baldwins though they were the first to be ordered. The seventy five locos were far more than were needed for the 750mm gauge railways actually completed in Patagonia and some spent many years in store before entering service. One of the purposes of the railway's rescue was to preserve employment, especially at El Maitén where it is by far the largest employer. The concession granted by the Argentine state to the two provincial governments is due to expire in 2024 and we must hope that it will be renewed on favourable terms.

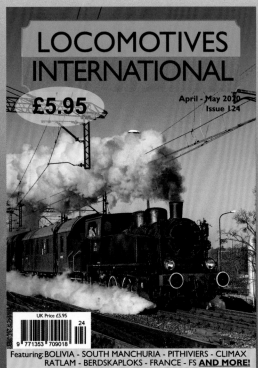
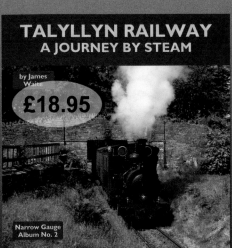